THE
SECRET RAPTURE
—Is it Scriptural?

Ralph Woodrow Evangelistic Association, Inc.
P.O. Box 21, Palm Springs, CA 92263-0021

International Standard Book Number: 0-916938-09-3

THE SECRET RAPTURE
Is it Scriptural?

by

Ralph Woodrow

Other books include:

Great Prophecies of the Bible
His Truth is Marching On!
The Babylon Connection?
Amazing Discoveries within the Book of Books
Noah's Flood, Joshua's Long Day, and Lucifer's Fall—What Really Happened?
Reckless Rumors, Misinformation, and Doomsday Delusions
Triumph Out of Tragedy

A complete catalog of books and/or information can be obtained by contacting:

RALPH WOODROW
P. O. BOX 21
PALM SPRINGS, CA 92263-0021

24-hour Phone Order/Message Line: (760) 323-9882
Toll-free (within the 48 states): (877) 664-1549
Fax: (760) 323-3982
E-mail: ralphwoodrow@earthlink.net
WebSite: www.ralphwoodrow.org

INTRODUCTION

All Christians generally believe that Christ will come again and believers will be caught up to meet the Lord in the air. But as to the *time* of this event (in relation to other events), there is not this general agreement. De Haan says that believers will be caught "up into heaven" *before* the tribulation period and that this "is the teaching of Revelation and *of the entire Bible."* On the other hand, Oswald Smith says: "There is not *a single verse in the Bible* that upholds the pre-tribulation theory....There is *no scripture* for a pre-tribulation rapture."

Regardless of *which* side we take, we will have to disagree with someone! In disagreeing, however, it is not our intention to be disagreeable. For the sake of clarity, we shall sometimes quote from various writers with whom we disagree. In doing this, it is not our purpose to cast any reflection upon their sincerity or calling. The other person may have rich stores of knowledge on other Christian doctrines (which we ourselves may lack) and it would be foolish to say, "I have no need of thee" (cf. 1 Corinthians 12:21).

We ask that these things be kept in mind as the reader pursues the pages that follow.

—RALPH EDWARD WOODROW

THE SECRET RAPTURE
Is it Scriptural?

We hear a lot today about the "rapture." It is preached and taught in positive terms on Christian radio and television programs. "The ultimate trip," as some call it, has been the theme of sensational movies. Bumper stickers carry slogans like: "In case of the Rapture, this vehicle will be unmanned," or "The Rapture: The only way to fly!"

Dramatic sermons tell how thousands of people will suddenly disappear into thin air. Cars will wreck, veer off the road, or plummet over cliffs, as drivers are raptured away. Planes will crash as Christian pilots go up in the rapture! Television programs will be interrupted as frantic voices give reports—a horrified husband says he and his wife were eating, when suddenly she disappeared right before his eyes. A mother reports seeing her baby instantly vanish from its crib. A Christian doctor who had just made the incision for major surgery, suddenly disappeared through the ceiling of the operating room!

While newspaper boys holler out headlines about "Millions Missing," church members (who missed the rapture!) will meet in emergency sessions, choosing new leadership, as they face the years ahead. The rapture has taken place! The trumpet of the Lord has sounded! And time continues on. *Is this the Scriptural description of the rapture?*

1

One can search all the way through the Bible and he will never find the word "rapture." The word itself is from the Latin *rapere,* the same word from which "rape" comes—meaning to seize, to take away. It seems to us that a more appropriate expression would be to simply say what the Bible says: that believers will be "caught up" to meet the Lord in the air. Nevertheless, the word rapture is now in common use, it is applied to the catching up of believers to meet the Lord, and so we will not refrain from using it here.

The issue before us is not the *word* "rapture." The doctrine of the second coming of Christ, which has been the "blessed hope" (Titus 2:13) of the church over the centuries, is not the issue. That believers will actually be caught up to meet the Lord in the air is not the issue. The issue before us is whether this catching up (or rapture) is *a separate and earlier event from the coming of the Lord.*

Christians who hold what is called the "dispensational" interpretation of prophecy, teach that the second coming of Christ will be in two stages: first, the RAPTURE (his coming *for* the saints), and then later the REVELATION (his coming *with* the saints). The interval between these two events, the great tribulation period, is commonly regarded as seven years. Verses like Revelation 1:7, "Behold, he cometh with clouds; and every eye shall see him," are applied to the REVELATION—his coming in power and glory. The RAPTURE, on the other hand, is presented as a *quiet, invisible,* and *secret* coming. The following quotations are representative of this view:

> His appearance in the clouds will be veiled to the human eye and NO ONE WILL SEE HIM. He will slip in, slip out; move in to get His jewels and slip out as under the cover of night.[1]

> Quickly and INVISIBLY, unperceived by the world, the Lord will come as a thief in the night and catch away His waiting saints.[2]

[The rapture] will be a SECRET appearing, and only the believers will know about it.[3]

In the Rapture, only the Christians see him—it's a mystery, a SECRET.[4] ⟿ *Hal Lindsay*

It will be a SECRET rapture—QUIET, NOISELESS, sudden as the step of the thief in the night. All that the world will know will be that multitudes at once have gone.[5]

In all respect to fine Christian people who believe this way, to us this is a strange doctrine. The very text on which the catching up (or rapture) is based implies just the opposite!

For the Lord himself shall descend from heaven with a SHOUT, with the VOICE of the archangel, and with the TRUMP of God: and the dead in Christ shall rise first: then we which are alive and remain shall be caught up together with them in the clouds, to meet the Lord in the air (1 Thessalonians 4:16,17).

To us, this text indicates anything but a quiet, secret rapture. Amid the sound of the Lord himself descending from heaven with a shout, the voice of the archangel, and the trumpet of God, there will be the sounds of praise and rejoicing from vast multitudes of saints as they are caught up to meet the Lord!

Suppose the Bible said: "The Lord *invisibly* shall descend from heaven, *quietly.*" What would we say to someone who told us this means he will come visibly and loudly? Would we not brand this twisting of words as unsound doctrine? Well, then, turn it around. The Bible actually does say, "The Lord *himself* shall descend from heaven with a *shout.*" To read "invisible" or "quiet" into this description is just as unsound. If Paul was trying to describe a secret event, he chose the wrong words!

Jesus actually warned against the idea of secrecy in connection with his second coming: "If any man shall say unto

3

you, Lo, here is Christ, or there; believe it not....If they shall say unto you...behold, he is in the *secret* chambers; believe it not. *For* as the lightning cometh out of the east, and shineth unto the west, so shall also the coming of the Son of man be" (Matt. 24:23-27).

THE TIME UNREVEALED

There is no indication anywhere in scripture that the second coming of Christ will be a secret event—only the *time* of the event is secret. Jesus stressed that men do not know the day or the hour of the second coming. It will be "as it was in the days of Noah" when people were eating, drinking, and getting married—not expecting destruction to fall. They "knew not UNTIL the flood came, and took them all away, so shall also the coming of the Son of man be" (Matthew 24:36-39). The wicked knew not until the flood came—but, obviously, when it came they knew it! It was no secret event. It was observed by believers and unbelievers.

"But know this," Jesus said, "if the good man of the house had known in what watch the *thief* would come, he would have watched, and would not have suffered his house to be broken up. Therefore be ye also ready: in such an hour as you think not the Son of man cometh" (Matthew 24:43,44). Christ's return will be like the coming of a thief in the sense we know not WHEN it will occur. There is nothing here to indicate a secret coming of Christ in which he will mysteriously take believers out of this world so that no one will know what happened to them or who took them. We should not think the Lord will prowl around like a thief, working in the dark, afraid of being discovered. The meaning is he will *come* "as a thief," not that he will *act* like a thief!

Scoffers will say, "Where is the promise of his coming?" But Peter assures us that the day of the Lord *will* come. We do not know *when*, however, for "the day of the Lord will come *as a thief in the night*" (2 Peter 3:10). But, again, the event itself will not be a quiet event, for Peter links it with a great noise! "The day of the Lord will come as a thief in the night; in the which the heavens shall pass away with a GREAT NOISE"!

In the noted rapture passage, after speaking of the Lord's coming with a shout, etc., Paul goes on to explain that we do not know *when* this will be, for that day will come as a thief in the night. "But of the times and seasons, brethren, you have no need that I write unto you. For yourselves know perfectly that the day of the Lord so cometh *as a thief in the night*" (1 Thessalonians 5:1,2). What is unknown and hidden? It cannot be that the coming of Christ, the event itself, will be secret. The context speaks of this as being glorious, open, noisy. It is the *time* that is unrevealed.

TRIUMPH IN TRIBULATION

Shortly before his death, Jesus spoke these words to his disciples: "In the world you shall have *tribulation...*" (John 16:33). The verses that follow record the prayer in which Jesus prayed for his disciples: "I pray *not* that thou shouldest *take them out of the world,* but that thou shouldest keep them from the evil" (John 17:15).

Though it would be no easy task to take a stand for Christ; though they would be persecuted; though in the world they would have tribulation; yet, Jesus did not pray that the church would be taken out of the world! The church was to remain *in* the world, but it would not be *of* the world.

Some might object, however, that Jesus was praying only for his immediate disciples of that time. But not so! "Neither pray I for these alone," he said, "but for them *also* which shall believe on me through their word" (verse 20).

5

Does this not include us today? Have not we believed on Christ as a result of the message handed down to us from those original disciples? Indeed we have. So Jesus was praying for us too! He said so. He prayed we would be kept from the evil of the world, but he did not pray that we would be taken out of the world—even though in the world we would have tribulation!

Let us suppose Jesus had told believers: "In the world there shall be tribulation...but I will pray that you will be taken out of the world." If Jesus said this, those who teach a pre-tribulation rapture would have a basis for their position—and this statement would no doubt be quoted *often* as a proof text. But since this is *not* what the verse says—but just the *opposite*— surely this should be regarded as evidence against the idea of a special, "secret" coming of Christ to take the church out of this world.

Instead of the church being taken out of the world, Jesus taught that it would remain in the world to accomplish a definite purpose: to preach the gospel. Jesus commissioned his disciples to "go...and teach all nations" and promised: "Lo, I am with you alway, even unto the *end* of the world [*aion*—age]" (Matthew 28:19,20).

UNTIL THE END

How long would the church be in the world fulfilling this divine commission? The implication is that this mission would continue until the end of the age. Surely this promise would be strange if God's plan was to remove the church seven years *before* that time! If, when the end of the age comes, the church would no longer be on earth, a promise such as this would be meaningless.

Earlier in the book of Matthew, Jesus made the same point. He gave a parable about a man who sowed good seed in his field, but an enemy sowed tares among the wheat. When the crop had grown, and the servants discovered what had happened, they asked if they should pull up the tares. To this the owner replied: "Let both grow together until the harvest: and in the time of harvest I will say to the reapers, Gather together first the tares, and bind them in bundles to burn them: but gather the wheat into my barn" (Matthew 13:24-30).

We are not left to speculate as to the correct meaning of the parable, for Jesus explained. The good seed, the wheat, is sown by "the Son of man"—Jesus Christ. The tares, the children of the wicked one, are sown by the enemy—"the devil." They are sown in the same field—"the world"—where both grow together until the harvest. "The harvest is the end of the world" (verses 37-39).

"As therefore the tares are gathered and burned in the fire; so shall it be in *the end of this world.* The Son of man shall send forth his angels, and they shall gather out of his kingdom all things that offend, and them which do iniquity; and shall cast them into a furnace of fire....*Then* shall the righteous shine forth as the sun in the kingdom of their Father" (verses 40-43). Plainly, the time of separation between those which do iniquity and the righteous is at the *end!*

Jesus said that "BOTH" would grow "TOGETHER" until the "END OF THE WORLD"—and *then* would be the harvest, producing the great separation. This is the Bible teaching. But the pre-tribulation rapture position, to be consistent, would have to say that BOTH will NOT grow together in the field until the end of the world, for they teach the wheat will be harvested sooner, being separated from the tares seven years BEFORE the end!

According to a footnote in the *Scofield Reference Bible,* "At the end of this age (v. 40) the tares are set apart for burning, but *first* the wheat is gathered into the barn."[6] But if anything might be implied as coming "first," it would be the judgment upon the wicked, for in the parable portion it said: "Gather together FIRST the tares" for destruction, "but gather the wheat into my barn" (Matthew 13:30). What? The scripture says: "First the tares." The note in the Scofield Bible says just the opposite! Such twisting of terms does not speak well for the pre-tribulation view.

Looking further in Matthew 13, Jesus likened the kingdom to a net which was cast into the sea. It gathered fish of every kind—some good, and some bad. Finally, the good were placed into vessels and the bad were cast away. *When* would this great separation occur? "So shall it be at the END of the world: the angels shall come forth, and sever the wicked from among the just, and shall cast them into the furnace of fire" (Matthew 13:47-50).

Jesus further likened the time of his return to the days of Lot. "As it was in the days of Lot; they did eat, they drank, they bought, they sold, they planted, they builded"—those common, routine things that people have been doing all along, not expecting any catastrophe—"but the same day that Lot went out of Sodom it rained fire and brimstone from heaven, and destroyed them all. Even thus shall it be in the day when the Son of man is revealed" (Luke 17:28-30). Lot, the believer, was spared. The unbelievers were destroyed. So when Christ returns, believers will be spared (caught up to meet the Lord in the air!) while that "same day" fiery destruction shall fall upon the world. There is nothing in this passage to suggest Lot went out of Sodom and then seven years later the fiery destruction fell. These things happened the *same day*.

Jesus likened his second coming to the destruction of the flood in the days of Noah. "But as the days of Noah were, so shall also the coming of the Son of man be. For as in the days that were before the flood they were eating and drinking, marrying and giving in marriage...and knew not until the flood came, and took them all away ["destroyed them all"—Luke 17:27]. *So* shall also the coming of the Son of man be. Then shall two be in the field; the one shall be taken and the other left" (Matthew 24:37-42).

ONE TAKEN AND THE OTHER LEFT

Sermons have sometimes been preached about "one shall be TAKEN, and the other LEFT," as though this meant believers would be *taken* up in the rapture and the unbelievers would be *left* to go through the tribulation period. But this can hardly be correct, for in the context it was the unbelievers who were taken away—by the destruction of the flood. In the days of Noah, the unbelievers "knew not until the flood came, and TOOK *them* all away; *so* shall also the coming of the Son of man be. Then shall two be in the field; the one shall be TAKEN, and the other left. Two women shall be grinding at the mill; the one shall be TAKEN, and the other left" (Matt. 24:39-42).

If we understand this in the light of the context, it will be *unbelievers* who will be *taken*—in death, by the "sudden destruction" that will accompany the Lord when he comes (1 Thessalonians 5:3). Those who believe in Christ will be *left*—their lives spared. True, they will be spared by being caught up—up above the sudden destruction—but this does not seem to be the primary point here.

Though the world was formerly destroyed by water, it was pointed out by Peter that the destruction the world now faces will be by *fire*. "The world that then was, being overflowed with water, perished: but the heavens and the earth, which are now, by the same word are kept in store, reserved unto fire" (2 Peter 3:6,7).

9

Peter had personally heard Jesus give the promise: "I will come again, and receive you unto myself" (John 14:3). Years passed and some began to scoff at this promise, saying: "Where is the promise of his coming?" To this Peter replied: "The Lord is not slack concerning his promise...the day of the Lord *will* come...IN THE WHICH the heavens shall pass away with a great noise, and the elements shall melt with fervent heat, the earth also and the works that are therein shall be burned up...all these things shall be dissolved" (2 Peter 3:10,11). Thus did he describe what Jesus had called "the end of the world."

Some believe such statements refer to a literal end of this planet. Others believe that the end of the age, but not necessarily the end of the planet, is the correct meaning. In Noah's day, it is pointed out, "the world that then was...perished"—but the planet remained; so likewise, "the heavens and the earth which are now"—this age—could end and the planet remain. But, either way, "the end of the world" is the *end*—there is a distinct finality here. There is no indication or room for the idea that time will continue on for another seven years after this. We do not believe it was a bad choice of words when the hymn writer said: "When the trumpet of the Lord shall sound and *time shall be no more...*"

Peter continues: "Seeing then that all these things shall be dissolved, what manner of person ought you to be in all holy conversation and godliness. *Looking for* and hasting unto the coming of the day of God, wherein the heavens being on fire shall be dissolved, and the elements shall melt with fervent heat?" (verses 11,12). Obviously Peter did not believe Christians would be taken out of the world seven years before the end. Why would he exhort them to be "looking for" the coming of the day of God when the heavens shall pass away? Why talk of the *end,* if their real hope was an event seven years earlier?

10

According to Peter, "the coming of the Lord"—"the day of the Lord" which will come "as a thief in the night"—is the time when the heavens shall pass away and the earth shall melt with fervent heat. And according to Paul, "the day of the Lord" which will come "as a thief in the night" (the *same* expression) is the time of the rapture:

> The Lord himself shall descend from heaven...we which are alive and remain shall be caught up...in the clouds, to meet the Lord in the air....But of the times and seasons [when this shall happen], brethren, you have no need that I write unto you. For yourselves know perfectly that the day of the Lord so cometh as a thief in the night. For when they shall say, Peace and safety; then sudden destruction cometh upon them...and they shall not escape (1 Thessalonians 4:16-5:3).

This passage, even though it spans two chapters, is all connected together. There is not the slightest hint that the rapture is a separate event from the destruction that will befall the world at the end.

"HEAVEN AND EARTH SHALL PASS AWAY"

Jesus expressed the finality of that day in these words: "Heaven and earth shall pass away....But of that day and hour knoweth no man, no, not the angels of heaven, but my Father only....Watch therefore: for you know not what hour your Lord doth come" (Matthew 24:36-42). If believers are to "watch" for that day—when heaven and earth shall pass away—it is evident they were not to be taken away seven years before.

Even the ancient Job implied the resurrection would not take place until the heavens shall pass away. "Man dieth, and wasteth away: yea, man giveth up the ghost, and where is he?...Man lieth down, and riseth not: *till the heavens be no more,* they shall not awake, nor be raised out of their sleep" (Job 14:10-12; 19:26,27). Expressions such as "till the heavens be no more," "the heavens shall pass away with

11

a great noise," "heaven and earth shall pass away," all seem to indicate the very end of things as we know them. Until that time, the dead shall not be resurrected.

Thus Martha believed Lazarus would "rise again in the resurrection AT THE LAST DAY" (John 11:24). This was not mere speculation on her part, for Jesus himself repeatedly spoke of the resurrection as being "AT THE LAST DAY" (John 6:39,40,44,54). Since the catching up or rapture occurs at the same time as the resurrection of the dead in Christ (1 Thessalonians 4:16,17), it is plain to see the rapture takes place at the last day, not seven years *before* the last day!

In the resurrection chapter (1 Corinthians 15), we are told that these things will occur "at the *last* trump: for the trumpet shall sound, and the dead shall be raised incorruptible, and we shall be changed" (verses 51,52). We know also, that on this "last day" at the "last trump," the "last enemy" shall be destroyed. Paul says "the last enemy that shall be destroyed is death" (1 Corinthians 15:26).

It will happen "in a moment, in the twinkling of an eye, at the last trump: for the trumpet shall sound, and the dead shall be raised...then"—at the resurrection and catching up—*"then* shall be brought to pass the saying that is written, Death is swallowed up in victory" (verses 52-54). According to dispensationalism, this happens before the tribulation—with seven years yet to go. But, then, what about people who will be killed after that, some of them being martyrs for Christ? The dispensational interpretation requires another resurrection at the end of the tribulation for them. Thus, if the last enemy is destroyed before the tribulation, it will have to be destroyed *again* after the tribulation! But put the destruction of the last enemy at the "last day," as the Bible does, and the last enemy is the *last* enemy!

What about tribulation martyrs? John saw people who refused to worship the beast and were beheaded. But "they lived and reigned with Christ a thousand years....*This is the first resurrection*. Blessed and holy is he that hath part in the first resurrection" (Revelation 20:4-6). Dispensationalism claims that these are people, martyred *after* the rapture of the church, who will be resurrected at the end of the tribulation period. But since the resurrection takes place at the rapture—as both sides agree—if the rapture takes place *before* the tribulation, how could a resurrection of tribulation martyrs be "the *first* resurrection"?

On the other hand, if the "first resurrection" is a bodily resurrection before the tribulation, these tribulation martyrs would be raised from the dead *before they were martyred!* But place the resurrection at the END, as the Bible does, and a scriptural harmony is obtained. Regardless of how we interpret Revelation 20:4-6, or whether the martyrs lived in the beginning centuries, during the Dark Ages, or the final years of this age, with the resurrection at the end, all are included without artificial additions to the word.

Until the rise of the secret rapture teaching (which is of comparatively recent origin), the idea of anyone being saved AFTER the coming of the Lord would have been considered strange indeed! Did the church *ever* in the first eighteen centuries of its history teach such a thing? Faithful preachers over the centuries voiced what Jesus and the apostles taught—about being sober, ready, watching, waiting for the Lord's return. Peter regarded the seeming delay in the Lord's coming as God's "longsuffering," allowing men additional time to repent (2 Peter 3:9). Obviously he did not believe people would be saved *after* the coming of the Lord!

But with the escape rapture teaching, there is not that urgency. After all, if one misses the rapture, as it is now taught, he can still get saved! According to *The Late Great Planet Earth,* not only will people be saved after the rapture, but this will be *the greatest time of evangelism the earth has ever known!* "After the Christians are gone God is going to reveal himself in a special way to 144,000 physical, literal Jews who are going to believe with a vengeance that Jesus is the Messiah. They are going to be 144,000 Jewish Billy Grahams turned loose on this earth—the earth will never know a period of evangelism like this period....They are going to have the greatest number of converts in all history."[7]

Imagine that—multitudes of people getting saved *after* the coming of the Lord (the rapture)! We can only say, this has never been the Biblical or historical position of the church. But now, some churches have announced an addition to their bylaws: a legal notice passing on the leadership of the church to backsliders and sinners! These, it is believed, will repent and be saved *after* the Lord comes in the rapture. If any had doubts before about Christianity, with millions "missing," they will now know for sure! They are to gather for an emergency board meeting—these people who *missed the rapture*—to elect new leaders so the work of the church can continue.

Some believe that after the pre-tribulation rapture, God will have a different plan of salvation! As one writer says, *"Now* we can be saved by the blood of Christ; but after the rapture, people will have to *give their own blood* to be saved—it will be a martyrs' route to heaven!" Another suggests that then people will be saved or lost on the basis of *how they treat the Jews.* A tract before me says: "If you should be left behind when Jesus comes...do not persecute the Jews...assist them in their distresses. For it may turn to be your salvation...those who have protected and cared for the Jews...who have hidden them, also fed and clothed them, will be found worthy of entrance into the kingdom age." This concept is based, supposedly, on the words of Jesus in the parable of the sheep and the goats. To the righteous—the sheep—Jesus will state they fed him, gave him drink, took him in as a stranger, and visited him in prison. And they will ask when they saw him in these circumstances. His reply: "Inasmuch as you have done it unto one of the least of these MY BRETHREN, you have done it unto me" (Matthew 25:40).

The dispensational belief, that "my brethren" means Jews during the tribulation period, introduces a third class of people into the parable—in addition to the sheep and goats. This is not justified, for Jesus was not speaking of a separate class of people, but simply spoke to the sheep, the righteous, as "my brethren." It is no different than if he had said: "My brethren, because you did it unto the least of these—the hungry, the thirsty, the sick, the oppressed," etc. The proof for this is evident, for the word "brethren" *only* appears when Jesus was speaking to the sheep. When he spoke to the goats, *the word "brethren" is absent,* as the following parallel shows:

TO THE SHEEP:	TO THE GOATS:
"Inasmuch as you have done it unto one of the least of these MY BRETHREN, you have done it unto me" (Matt. 25:40).	"Inasmuch as you did it not to one of the least of these, you did it not to me" (Matt. 25:45).

Once the entire passage is read, the point will become obvious. If "my brethren" meant a separate class of people—rather than a simple form of address to those termed "sheep"—it should have appeared in the second portion also. Besides, Christ's "brethren" could hardly mean a group of Jews—in a *fleshly* sense—for Jesus himself said (as also recorded in Matthew) that *all* who do the will of the Father are his brethren (Matthew 12:48-50).

15

Over and over the Bible has stressed that the coming of the Lord will suddenly occur, that the time is unknown, that no man knows the day or hour of the end of the age. But if the rapture is an event to take place seven years *before* the end, *thousands* of people would be able to determine the *exact* date! All they would have to do is count seven years from the time all babies and Christians suddenly came up "missing."

If any questions remained, a trip to the cemetery would provide absolute proof that the rapture had occurred. By digging down into the graves of known Christians—a godly grandmother, a dedicated pastor, or a baby that had recently died—and finding their caskets empty, it would be evident the resurrection had taken place. It would not take long for thousands to know what had happened—and to figure the exact date for the end of the age. But since the scriptures teach that no man knows the day or hour when the end will come, it is evident that the rapture is not a separate event seven years before the end.

The description Jesus gave of his return rules out the idea of two separate events. "The Son of man shall come in the glory of his Father with his angels; and *then* he shall reward *every man* according to his works" (Matthew 16:27). This can not be a secret coming of Christ *alone,* for he comes in glory with the angels. It is at this time every man is rewarded. This can hardly fit the idea of the rapture being an earlier event, for in that case many would have already been caught up and rewarded!

"Whosoever therefore shall be ashamed of me and of my words in this adulterous and sinful generation, of him also shall the Son of man be ashamed, when he cometh in the glory of his Father with the holy angels" (Mark 8:38). If there had been an earlier coming of Christ, alone, in a secret rapture, whether he would be ashamed of people or not

16

would have already taken place. Why would he speak of these things in connection with his coming in glory with the angels?

The Christians at Thessalonica were enduring "persecutions and tribulations" and were being "troubled" by unbelievers (2 Thess. 1:4,7). But Paul encouraged them with the truth that they would be given "rest" from their troubles "when the Lord Jesus shall be revealed from heaven *with his mighty angels,* in flaming fire taking vengeance on them that know not God," for "he shall come to be glorified in his saints" (see 2 Thessalonians 1:7-10).

In this passage—as in the others—the reward of the righteous and the destruction that shall befall the wicked are interwoven with each other as to time, *both* occurring at the coming of the Lord. We notice also that when Jesus comes for the deliverance of his troubled saints, he comes in "flaming fire." No secret rapture here!

When will the Lord render vengeance to the wicked on one hand, and comfort to the saints on the other? The answer is clear: "WHEN the Lord Jesus shall be revealed from heaven with his mighty angels, in flaming fire, taking vengeance on them which know not God." The time of his being glorified in his saints is also the time when destruction will fall on the wicked. There is no interval of seven years between the two.

TWO STAGES OF ONE SECOND COMING?

The author's own study of the Bible, including Bible prophecy, began at an early age. While in my teens, I was stirred, like the people at Berea, to "search the scriptures daily" to see, for myself, what the Bible says (Acts 17:11). Most of the Christians I knew back then had been influenced by the "dispensational" interpretation of prophecy —that Jesus was coming back two more times: first in a

17

secret rapture, then seven years later in glory and power at the end of the age. I knew Jesus had come the first time, and that "unto them that look for him shall he appear the *second* time without sin unto salvation" (Hebrews 9:28), but where did the scriptures teach a *third* coming of Christ? Most, of course, did not use the term third coming; it fit better to say there were "two stages" of the one second coming.

This wording seemed awkward to me—like something added to make a theory fit. If the rapture is a separate "stage" from the coming of Christ in power and glory, one wonders how each "stage" could be the *second* coming? If they are separate and distinct events—separated by several years—a coming that follows the second coming would be a third! But the scriptures never speak of a third coming, or of "comings" (plural), and the term "two second comings" is self-contradictory.

In an attempt to explain this difficulty, some dispensational writers go so far as to argue that the "rapture" is not the COMING of the Lord! One puts it this way: "Strictly speaking the rapture is NOT THE SECOND COMING AT ALL. The second coming is the visible, local, bodily appearing of Christ in the clouds of heaven as he returns to this earth...in power and great glory."[8] Another says: "The thrilling event which will both mark the end of the day of grace and open the door for the Great Tribulation is the rapture....Specifically speaking, THIS IS NOT THE SECOND COMING OF CHRIST. Rather this is the rapture, or the catching up, of the true church."[9]

But attempting to make the catching up a *separate* and *earlier* event from the coming of Christ, is glaringly inconsistent with the wording of scripture. Jesus said, "Be ye therefore also ready: for in such an hour as you think not the Son of man COMETH" (Matthew 24:44). Why would Jesus warn about being ready for the COMING of the Son of man, if the rapture takes place *before* his coming?

18

Jesus said: "Occupy till I COME" (Luke 19:13). How could the church occupy until he comes, if the church will be raptured away seven years before his coming? Jesus said: "I will COME again, and receive you unto myself" (John 14:3). Plainly it is when Jesus comes that he receives his people unto himself. The receiving is not seven years before his coming!

In perfect harmony with these teachings of Jesus, the apostles admonished: "Be patient then, brethren, unto the COMING of the Lord...for yet a little while, and he that shall COME will COME, and will not tarry" (James 5:7; Hebrews 10:36,37). Again, why exhort the brethren to be patient unto the COMING of the Lord, if their real hope was a rapture *before* his coming?

Paul speaks of Christians as "waiting for the COMING of our Lord Jesus Christ" (1 Corinthians 1:7). If he believed Christians would be caught up to heaven in a secret rapture seven years before the Lord's coming, why didn't he speak of Christians as waiting for that? Paul certainly did not consider the rapture a separate event. Even in the "rapture" passage, he comes right out and calls the catching up of believers "the COMING of the Lord"! (1 Thessalonians 4:15). In view of these things, we find it very strained for writers to make statements that the rapture is not the coming of the Lord.

Some may ask: What about the meaning of the *Greek* words that are used to describe the second coming? One writer says: "The TWO phases of Christ's second coming are *clearly* distinguished in the Greek. The 'parousia'...is his coming for his saints....The 'apokalupsis' (the revealing, unveiling, making manifest) is his coming with his saints."[10] But, as we shall see, instead of the Greek words indicating two separate events, the various words are actually used *interchangeably!*

19

The following is a list of six Greek words that describe the second coming of Christ, the specific meaning of each, and a representative verse in which each word is used:

1. *Parousia* (the personal presence of one who comes and arrives): "Be patient...unto the *coming* of the Lord" (James 5:7).

2. *Apokalupsis* (appearing, revelation): "The Lord shall be *revealed* from heaven with his mighty angels" (2 Thess. 1:7).

3. *Epiphaneia* (manifestation, glory): "The *appearing* of our Lord Jesus Christ" (1 Timothy 6:14).

4. *Phaneroo* (to render apparent): "When he shall *appear*, we shall be like him" (1 John 3:2).

5. *Erchomai* (the act of coming, to come from one place to another): "Occupy till I *come*" (Luke 19:13).

6. *Heko* (the point of arrival): "Hold fast till I *come*" (Revelation 2:25).

The first word on our list, *parousia,* stresses the actual personal presence of one that has come and arrived. Nothing in this word conveys the idea of *secrecy.* It was in common use, as when Paul spoke of the "coming *[parousia]* of Titus" (2 Cor. 7:6), the "coming *[parousia]* of Stephanas" (1 Cor. 16:17), and of his own "coming *[parousia]*" to Philippi (Philippians 1:26).

Paul used this word in the noted rapture passage which speaks of "the coming *[parousia]* of the Lord" when believers will be caught up to meet the Lord in the air (1 Thessalonians 4:15-17). But Paul's use of this word here can hardly mean a separate event from the Lord's coming at the end of the age, for in his second letter to the Thessalonians, he places the *parousia* AFTER the reign of the man of sin—not before! Speaking of "the coming *[parousia]* of our Lord" and "our gathering together unto him," Paul says "the Lord shall destroy [the man of sin] with the brightness of his coming *[parousia]*" (2 Thessalonians 2:8).

Peter, like Paul, spoke of the Lord's "coming *[parousia]*" at the end of the age, when "the heavens shall pass away with a great noise, and the elements shall melt with fervent heat." He exhorted Christians to "look for...the coming [*parousia*] of the day of God, wherein the heavens being on fire shall be dissolved, and the elements shall melt with fervent heat" (2 Peter 3:4-12). In none of these instances could *parousia* mean a pre-tribulation rapture.

It should also be noted here, the plural form of the word *parousia* is not used in connection with the Lord's coming. The definite article is consistently used. It is not *a* coming of the Lord, but *the* coming of the Lord.

Peter told Christians to "hope to the *end* for the grace that is to be brought unto you at the REVELATION [*apokalupsis*] of Jesus Christ" (1 Peter 1:13). Those who teach that Christ comes first in the RAPTURE, then seven years later in the REVELATION, face serious difficulties here. It would not be necessary for Christians to hope to the end for the grace to be brought to them at the REVELATION of Christ, if, in reality, this grace was to be given at a separate rapture seven years before! In the immediate context, Peter spoke of Christians being "found unto praise and honor and glory at the APPEARING [*apokalupsis—revelation*] of Jesus Christ" (verse 7). Christians are "waiting for the coming [*apokalupsis—revelation*] of our Lord Jesus Christ" (1 Corinthians 1:7). But, again, why would Christians be waiting for the "revelation" if the "rapture" comes seven years sooner?

According to the Bible, the *apokalupsis*—the revelation of Christ—is when Christians will be gathered; this is when they meet the Lord; this is the day for which they are waiting. The rapture, then, cannot be one event and the revelation a later event. Instead of two phases being "clearly distinguished in the Greek" by the terms *parousia* and *apokalupsis,* both are used in a way that points to one event, the second coming of Christ at the end of the age.

21

Another word used to describe the return of Christ, *epiphaneia*, speaks of manifestation and glory that will accompany our Lord. No one applies this to a secret, pretribulation coming, for Christ will slay the man of sin "with the brightness *[epiphaneia]* of his coming" (2 Thess. 2:8). Bearing this in mind, notice that Christians are to "...keep this commandment without spot, unrebukeable, until the appearing *[epiphaneia]* of our Lord Jesus Christ: which in his times he shall *show*...the King of kings and Lord of lords" (1 Tim. 6:14,15). Why would Christians be exhorted to keep the commandment until the *epiphaneia* —the glorious appearing—if the rapture was seven years before this?

The fourth word on our list, *phaneroo*, means to render apparent, referring to the open power and glory of Christ's coming. "When the chief Shepherd shall appear *[phaneroo]*, you shall receive a crown of glory" (1 Peter 5:4). If Christians had been raptured and crowned at an earlier coming of Christ, what sense would these words make? As John said: "We know that, when he shall appear *[phaneroo]*, we shall be like him; for we shall see him as he is" (1 John 3:2). As Christians it is when Christ shall come and appear—be rendered apparent—we shall be like him. Nothing here about an invisible coming!

Instead of the Greek terms indicating two separate events, just the opposite is the case. They are used interchangeably. Jesus said: "But as the days of Noah were, so shall also the COMING *[parousia]* of the son of man be" (Matt. 24:37). Luke's account of the *same* passage says: "As it was in the days of Noah...even thus shall it be in the day when the son of man is REVEALED *[apokalupsis]*" (Luke 17:26,30). "Therefore be ye also ready; for in such an hour as you think not the son of man COMETH *[erchomai]*" (Matt. 24:44). Here, then, *parousia, apokalupsis,* and *erchomai* are all used of the same event.

Erchomai, in turn, is used to describe the same event as *heko:* "For yet a little while, and he that shall COME *[erchomai]* will COME *[heko],* and will not tarry" (Hebrews 10:37). *Heko* and *parousia* are used together: "Where is the promise of his COMING *[parousia]*?....The day of the Lord will COME *[heko]* as a thief in the night" (2 Peter 3:10). *Parousia* and *epiphaneia* are linked together: the man of sin will be destroyed by the "BRIGHTNESS *[epiphaneia]*" of Christ's "COMING *[parousia]*" (2 Thessalonians 2:8). And, we know that the *parousia* is the *phaneroo,* for both expressions are used together: "And now, little children, abide in him; that, when he shall APPEAR *[phaneroo],* we may have confidence, and not be ashamed before him at his COMING *[parousia]*" (1 John 2:28).

Thus we see that *all* of these Greek words are used *interchangeably.* As in English, the different words present varied shades of meaning. But trying to split the second coming of Christ into two "stages" or "comings" on a supposed distinction in Greek terms is completely artificial.

When Jesus ascended into heaven and his disciples stood watching, two angels said: "You men of Galilee, why stand gazing up into heaven? this same Jesus, which is taken up from you into heaven, shall so come *in like manner* as you have *seen* him go into heaven" (Acts 1:11). The fact that they did not see him go into heaven in two ascensions, strongly suggests his return will not be in two stages.

COMING "FOR" AND "COMING" WITH THE SAINTS

What about the argument commonly given—that since the Lord will come "with" his saints (Jude 14), there must be an earlier coming of the Lord "for" the saints to take them to heaven? Actually, the Bible never uses the expression "coming FOR the saints." And the rapture text, instead of saying believers will be raptured to heaven, actually says

23

they will be "caught up...in the *clouds,* to meet the Lord in the *air"* (1 Thessalonians 4:16,17). Where they go, after meeting the Lord in the clouds, is not explained in this text.

When we are told that believers will rise to "MEET" the Lord in the air, the word is *apantesis.* It was used to describe the coming of a king or governor to visit a city, who, as he approached would be met by citizens who would then escort him on the last part of his journey into the city. If it has that same meaning here, as the Lord descends from heaven, believers will rise "to meet the Lord in the air," in order to *come* with him. This would not require a separate coming. *Apantesis* appears again in the parable of the ten virgins who "took their lamps, and went forth to MEET the bridegroom" (Matthew 25:1,6). After they went out to "meet" him, they returned "with him."

One final use of the word *apantesis* appears in connection with Paul's journey to Rome. "When the brethren heard of us, they came to MEET us as far as Appii forum...and when we came to Rome..." (Acts 28:14-16). Suppose the men who went to meet Paul told of their plans—that they heard Paul was coming to Rome and they were going to meet him. Whether they explained it or not, their going to meet him would imply they were coming back with him. None would understand this to mean they would meet Paul, go back to where he had been, spend some time there, in order to finally come *with* him to Rome!

The late Oswald J. Smith, noted missionary statesman, pastor, and song writer, sums it up in these words: "I learned, too, that the word for 'meet' in 1 Thessalonians 4...meant 'returning with' and not 'remaining at' the place of meeting. When the brethren from Rome met Paul, they immediately returned to the city with him. When the virgins met the bridegroom they accompanied him back to the wedding. When the saints meet Christ in the air...they will

24

return *with* him....There is no secret rapture. That theory must be deliberately read into the passage."[11]

But regardless of how we take the word "meet" or the expression "coming with," Jude 14 can add no weight to the two-stage position. There are good reasons to believe the "saints" mentioned in this verse are the ANGELS who come with the Lord! "Behold, the Lord cometh with ten thousands of his saints," (Jude 14). The word translated "saints" is *hagios*, meaning simply "holy," or in this case, "holy [ones]." The word usage itself could indicate angels or men, but in this context we believe angels are meant.

The *Pulpit Commentary* says: "The 'ten thousands of his saints' is better rendered 'ten thousands of his holy ones'....For the 'holy ones' here intended are the *angels*."[12] This fits perfectly with the words of Jesus who spoke of coming with the holy angels—holy being the same word, *hagios,* used in Jude 14. "The Son of man shall come in his glory, and all the holy *[hagios]* angels with him..." (Matthew 25:31). "Whosoever shall be ashamed of me...of him also shall the Son of man be ashamed, when he cometh...with the holy *[hagios]* angels" (Mark 8:38).

The expression "ten thousands of saints" (used in Jude 14) also appears in Deuteronomy 33:2, a passage generally regarded as referring to angels: "The Lord came from Sinai, and rose up from Seir unto them; he shined forth from mount Paran, and he came with ten thousands of saints." Again, the *Pulpit Commentary* points out that a better translation would be "ten thousands of holy ones," the reference being to angels.[13]

The *Matthew Henry Commentary* makes the same point: "His appearance was glorious: he shone forth like the sun when he goes forth in his strength. Even Seir and Paran, two mountains at some distance, were illuminated by the

25

divine glory which appeared on Mount Sinai....He came with his holy angels....Hence the law is said to be given by the disposition of angels, Acts 7:53; Hebrews 2:2."[14]

If the expression "ten thousands of saints" referred to angelic beings in Deuteronomy, it is not inconsistent to believe the *same* expression can mean angelic beings in Jude 14. This position finds further support in the context, for these holy ones are associated with Christ in executing judgment upon the ungodly. "Behold, the Lord cometh with ten thousands of his *hagios* [holy ones], to execute judgment upon...all that are ungodly" (Jude 14,15). We believe this will be the job of angelic beings, not that of Christians. As the scriptures say: "At the end of the world...the *angels* shall come forth, and sever the wicked from among the just, and shall cast them into the furnace of fire" (Matthew 13:49,50). "The Lord Jesus shall be revealed from heaven with his mighty *angels,* in flaming fire taking vengeance on them that know not God" (2 Thessalonians 1:7).

IS IT SCRIPTURAL?

The author once read the entire New Testament through for the express purpose of listing all scriptures that teach the return of Christ will be in two stages. (All of the verses I found are listed on page 55 of this book.) My conclusion was the same as Oswald J. Smith: "We might go through all the writers of the New Testament, and we would fail to discover any indication of the so-called 'two-stages' of our Lord's coming....There is no verse in the Bible that even mentions it."[15]

This point is known and admitted by men of varied denominational backgrounds. Renowned Biblical expositor, G. Campbell Morgan, said: "The idea of a separate and secret coming of Christ is...without any Biblical basis whatsoever."[16] Or consider the following statement by Pat

Robertson: "If we assume that the tribulation will be a future worldwide time of persecution, then I must say that Christians will indeed go through it. I do not find in the Bible the teaching that Christians will be 'raptured' prior to the tribulation....The Bible teaches two comings of Jesus—one his birth; the second, his coming again in triumph. There is no third coming for a secret rapture."[17]

Even men who believe in a pre-tribulation rapture have sometimes admitted there is no scripture for it. Wilfrid Meloon mentions how he once heard Charles Fuller say on his radio program, "There is not one verse in the entire New Testament which teaches a pre-tribulation rapture of the church—but, I still believe it."[18] He loved Charles Fuller, but was puzzled by this statement. How important, how major, can a doctrine be—whatever it is—if "not one verse" in the Bible teaches it?

DISPENSATIONAL PROOF TEXTS

Though the two-stage teaching is not actually mentioned in the Bible, Christians who believe this way feel it is justified by indirect evidence from certain "proof texts" we will now consider. First, Revelation 4:1:

After this I [John] looked, and, behold, a door was opened in heaven: and the first voice which I heard was as it were of a trumpet talking with me; which said, Come up hither, and I will show thee things which must be hereafter.

Scofield says: "This call seems *clearly* to indicate the fulfillment of 1 Thessalonians 4:14-17 [the rapture]. The word 'church' does not again occur in the Revelation till all is fulfilled."[19] De Haan, echoing this view, says: "This brief passage from Revelation is one of the shortest yet one of the *clearest* pictures in scripture of the rapture of the church."[20]

Since the word "church" does not appear in Revelation, chapters 4-18, the dispensational claim is that the church is absent from the earth during this time, and does not come into the picture again until chapter 19, which tells of the marriage supper and the coming of Christ as King of kings. But if the absence of the word "church" can prove the church is absent in chapters 4-18, we would have to conclude the church is also absent in chapter 19, for the word does not appear in that chapter either! Nor does it appear in chapter 20—or chapter 21! Only in a closing remark in the final chapter do we find these words: "I Jesus have sent mine angel to testify unto you these things in the *churches*"—not the universal church as a whole, but the seven churches of Asia (Revelation 22:16).

While the word "church" does not appear after chapter three until the last part of Revelation, the church is *not* absent in those chapters. In Revelation 13:7, we read that the beast would "make war with the saints." Verse 10 mentions the "patience and faith of the saints"—patience and faith in the midst of persecution! The "saints" are again mentioned in chapter 16, verse 6. In chapter 17 we read about the Babylonian woman "drunken with the blood of the saints" (verse 6) and that "in her was found the blood of the saints" (Revelation 18:24).

The dispensational position is that the saints mentioned in these chapters are not church saints, but tribulation saints. Yet when we find the word "saints" in chapter 19, we are told this refers to the church! "The marriage of the Lamb is come, and his wife hath made herself ready. And to her was granted that she should be arrayed in fine linen, clean and white: for the fine linen is the righteousness of saints" (Revelation 19:7,8). The Scofield footnote says: "The 'Lamb's wife' here is the 'bride,' the *Church*."[21] But to be consistent, if the saints in Revelation 19 are church saints, how can some rightly argue that the saints mentioned in the chapter before (chapter 18), the chapter before that (chapter

28

17), the chapter before that (chapter 16), and chapter 13 are some different kind of saints? This is arbitrary.

The rapture is not the subject of Revelation 4:1, it simply records the experience of John—in spirit—being taken into the heavenly realm. This does not prove we should look for the church in heaven any more than his being taken into the wilderness, to Babylon, would prove the church was there! (Revelation 17:3-5). As the various scenes of Revelation unfold, John is represented as being different places—on the earth (he sees an angel "come down [not go down] from heaven"—Revelation 10:1, 18:1), he measures what is, apparently, an earthly temple, for its courts are trodden down by Gentiles (Revelation 11:1), he stands upon the sand of the sea and watches a beast rise from its waters (Revelation 13:1). Plainly, John cannot be a *consistent* type of the church in heaven during these chapters.

KEPT FROM THE "HOUR OF TEMPTATION"

Another dispensational proof text, also from the book of Revelation, contains the words of Jesus to the church at Philadelphia:

> Because thou hast kept the word of my patience, I also will keep thee from the hour of temptation, which shall come upon all the world, to try them that dwell upon the earth (Revelation 3:10).

Those who use this verse in defense of the secret rapture position must assume the "hour of temptation" is the same as what they call "The Great Tribulation Period" at the end of this age. They must then assume that being kept from this temptation requires being raptured out of this world!

In its primary application, this promise would have pertained to the church of Philadelphia, located in Asia Minor, in the first century. Were the people of this church kept from a world-wide time of temptation? As sure as the promise is true, they were. But this did not require a rapture. We believe they were kept by the power and grace of God. If God fulfilled his promise to them, the "hour of temptation"—whatever might be the precise meaning of this expression—would have occurred in their day. This could hardly offer proof for a secret rapture to escape a great tribulation period 2,000 years later.

Some believe the seven churches of Asia represent seven successive ages of the church, extending from the first century to the rapture. If so, then the message to the church at Philadelphia could not refer to the rapture, for Philadelphia would be the sixth church in the succession, not the last (the seventh)! If the message to the Philadelphia church proves an escape rapture, the church ages would have to be 1,2,3,4,5,7,6!

We believe Christians can be kept from an hour of temptation—in any age—without being raptured out of the world! This principle can be established by comparing the following scriptures:

> Because thou hast *kept* the *word* of my patience, I also will *keep* thee from the hour of *temptation,* which shall come upon all the world, to try them that dwell upon the earth. (Revelation 3:10).

> They have *kept* thy *word....*I pray not that thou shouldest take them out of the world, but that thou shouldest *keep* them from the *evil.* (John 17:6,15).

Both of these passages are the words of Jesus. Both were recorded by John. The people in both passages have kept the word. Because they have kept the word, God will "keep them." In one passage they are kept from the hour of *temptation;* in the other, they are kept from *evil.* These are closely related terms, as in the Lord's prayer: "Lead us not into temptation, but deliver us from evil" (Matthew 6:13). If believers can be kept from the evil of the world without being taken out of the world—as in the one passage—it is certain they don't have to be raptured away from temptation in the other.

Though Revelation 3:10 probably had a specific meaning and fulfillment to the Philadelphia church of the first century, here also is a promise of God's keeping power in any hour of temptation, in any century, any year, any day—not just the last seven years of this age.

Paul wrote: "There hath no temptation taken you but such as is common to man, but God...will not suffer you to be *tempted* above that you are able; but will with the temptation also make a way of *escape* that you may be able to bear it" (1 Corinthians 10:12,13). "The Lord knoweth how to deliver the godly out of temptations" (2 Peter 2:9). Jabez prayed: *"Keep* me from evil...and God granted him that which he requested" (1 Chronicles 4:10). And we, today, can also be *"kept* by the power of God through faith unto salvation" (1 Peter 1:5), for God "is able to *keep* you from falling" (Jude 24). God's keeping power and escape from temptation can be provided without a secret rapture!

One more text should be noticed here:

Watch therefore and *pray* always, that you may be accounted worthy to ESCAPE all these things that shall come to pass, and to stand before the Son of man (Luke 21:36).

Here is a verse about praying for "escape," but again, nothing about the church being raptured out of this world in order for this to be accomplished! In the prayer of Jesus, he said: "I pray NOT that thou shouldest take them out of the world, but that thou shouldest keep them from the evil" (John 17:15). Would Jesus pray one way and tell the disciples to pray another way?

With what is this word "escape" connected? Is it escape from a *period of time*—a dispensational great tribulation during the last seven years of this age? It does not say so. A look at the context shows the reference is to "THAT DAY," the time believers will be gathered to meet the Lord in the air and destruction shall fall upon the world.

> Heaven and earth shall pass away [the end of the age]...take heed to yourselves, lest at any time your hearts be overcharged with surfeiting, and drunkenness, and cares of this life, and so THAT DAY come upon you unawares. For as a snare shall it come on all them that dwell on the face of the whole earth. Watch therefore, and pray always, that you may be accounted worthy to escape all these things that shall come to pass, and to stand before the Son of man" (Luke 21:33-36).

If believers were to no longer be on the earth—if they were to be raptured away seven years before the end—how could "that day" possibly come upon them unawares?

Jesus promised that those who are prayerfully watching and not overcharged with eating and drinking will escape the destruction of THAT DAY. The same basic message was presented by Paul:

> THE DAY of the Lord so cometh as a thief in the night. For when they shall say, Peace and safety; then *sudden destruction* cometh upon them as travail upon a woman with child; and they shall *not escape.* But you, brethren, are not in darkness that THAT DAY should overtake you as a thief. You are all the children of the light...we are not of the night....Therefore let us not sleep, as do others; but let us *watch*...for God hath not appointed us to wrath, but to obtain salvation by our Lord Jesus Christ (1 Thessalonians 5:1-9).

Notice how this passage also mentions THAT DAY. It will bring "sudden destruction" upon unbelievers, "and they shall *not* escape." Christians, however, will escape. They are not appointed to wrath. They will be caught up in the clouds to meet the Lord in the air, while destruction falls on the earth below.

Did the early Christians believe the rapture could occur at *any* moment? Or did they believe there were certain things that would be fulfilled *first?*

We believe there is conclusive proof in the New Testament that the early church did *not* hold the any moment teaching. Jesus pointed out that no man knows the time of his return and that we should live a life of watchfulness and obedience at all times. However, Jesus himself taught certain things would happen first.

When Jesus told his disciples of the second coming, he was still with them *in person*. Obviously the ascension had to precede the return. And before his ascension, of course, was to be Calvary: "First must he suffer many things, and be rejected of this generation" (Luke 17:25).

Jesus told his disciples that after his ascension, he would send the Holy Spirit upon them. This would take place, obviously, *before* Christ would come again. Thus, prior to Pentecost, we see the disciples waiting—not for the second coming of Christ—but the coming of the Holy Spirit to endue them with power. Being filled with the Holy Spirit they were to go into all the world and teach all nations (Acts 1:8). Time had to be allowed for travel, preaching, baptizing, instructing converts, etc. Surely Jesus would not return before they had time to do what he had commissioned them to do!

Jesus predicted the destruction of Jerusalem and told his disciples: "When you see Jerusalem compassed with armies, then know that the desolation thereof is nigh. Then let them which are in Judea flee to the mountains" (Luke 21:21). At the second coming of Christ, there will be no need for Christians to flee into the mountains, for they will be caught up to meet the Lord in the air! The destruction of Jerusalem, then, was to be an event *before* the second coming of Christ. Living on this side of the fulfillment, we know Jerusalem was destroyed in 70 A.D.

PETER'S DEATH

Jesus also explained that Peter would grow old and die—BEFORE the second coming! "When thou shalt be old," Jesus said to Peter, "thou shalt stretch forth thy hands, and another shall gird thee, and carry thee whither thou wouldest not. This spake he, signifying by what death he would glorify God" (John 21:18,19; cf. 2 Peter 1:14). Then Peter asked if John would live to see the coming of the Lord. Jesus replied: "If I will that he tarry till I come, what is that to thee? follow thou me." On the basis of this statement, a saying spread "among the brethren, that that disciple [John] should not die: yet Jesus said not unto him, he shall not die; but, If I will that he tarry till I come, what is that to thee?" (John 21:20-23). Whether John would live to see the second coming was not answered, but in the case of Peter, it was definitely stated he would grow old and die before the Lord's return.

We believe the early Christians lived in an expectation and hope of the second coming; for, whether alive at that time, or because of the resurrection, they would all ultimately share in the glory of that day! But they did not believe his coming would be at any moment; they knew certain things would happen first.

Writing to the Thessalonians, Paul spoke of the resurrection and catching up of believers to meet the Lord in the air (1 Thessalonians 4:16,17). Later, some confusion developed in their minds about this glorious event, and in his second epistle, Paul clarified the matter. His remarks show he did not hold the any-moment position:

> Now we beseech you, brethren, by [concerning] the coming of
> our Lord Jesus Christ, and by [concerning] our *gathering to-
> gether* unto him, that you be not soon shaken in mind, or be
> troubled, neither by spirit, nor by word, nor by letter as from
> us, as that the day of Christ is at hand. Let no man deceive
> you by any means: for that day shall *not* come, except there
> come a falling away *first,* and that man of sin be revealed, the
> son of perdition. (2 Thessalonians 2:1-3).

Here, then, two things are mentioned that Christians
would witness *before* the day of Christ's coming to gather
believers unto himself. There would be a falling away and
the man of sin would be revealed. Concerning these very
things, the inspired apostle said: "Let no man deceive you"!
Let us beware, then, of a teaching which says the church
will be raptured to heaven BEFORE the man of sin is revealed. According to Paul, the order of events would be: (1)
a falling away, (2) the man of sin would be revealed, and
(3) the coming of Christ and our gathering together unto
him. It is plain. But according to the any moment view, instead of these events being in this order, they would have to
be: 3, then 1, and then 2! That is: (3) the coming of Christ
and our gathering together unto him, (1) a falling away, and
(2) the man of sin revealed: 3,1,2, or perhaps 3,2,1, instead
of 1,2,3!

In an attempt to justify this reversal of events, some
teach that the falling away is a departure—the departure of
the church in the rapture! But the word translated "falling
away" is *apostasia,* meaning apostasy, a departure from the
truth, a well established meaning. To attempt to make "falling away" mean "catching up" shows how hard pressed the
dispensational arrangement is!

Paul said believers would witness certain events first:
the falling away, the man of sin would be revealed, and then
the gathering together to meet the Lord at his coming. But if
the falling away meant the rapture—an exodus of believers

from the world—they would not witness the events that followed, for they would not be here! Paul's words would have no bearing on the point he was making.

Being "troubled" with "persecutions and tribulations," the believers at Thessalonica wondered if the day of Christ was not right "at hand" (2 Thessalonians 1,2). If Paul had believed in the any moment position, here was his perfect opportunity to encourage them with the teaching that Jesus was coming *soon*—at any moment. He might have written something like this: "Now we beseech you, brethren, concerning the coming of our Lord Jesus Christ and our gathering together unto him, that you be not soon shaken in mind, for *nothing needs to happen first.* That day shall come *before* the falling away and *before* the man of sin is revealed. Yes, our gathering together unto him could happen *at any moment!*"

But to the contrary, this was *not* his answer. Instead, he explained there would be a falling away, and the man of sin would be revealed, before the day of Christ! There can be no mistake that "the day of Christ" refers to the rapture, for it is used in reference to "our gathering together unto him" (2 Thess. 2). Christians are "waiting" for the "day of the Lord Jesus Christ" (1 Cor. 1:7-9). It is "in the day of the Lord Jesus" that they will be gathered and "rejoice" at seeing each other (2 Cor. 1:14). The "good work" begun in Christians must continue "until the day of the Lord Jesus Christ" (Phil. 1:6). Paul admonished the Philippian believers to be "sincere and without offence" until "the day of Christ" (verse 10), when he would see them and rejoice that his labor had not been in vain (Phil. 2:16). All of these verses plainly show that the "day of Christ" is the time when believers are gathered to meet Christ.

Scofield, attempting to deal with the glaring problem dispensationalism faces here, says that the King James Version "has 'day of Christ,' 2 Thessalonians 2:2, incorrectly, for 'day of the Lord'."[22] Apparently some ancient manuscripts have it one way and some another. But what difference does this make? We use the expression "the coming of the *Lord*" when referring to "the coming of *Christ*." Why try to make the New Testament expression "the day of the *Lord*" mean something different than "the day of *Christ*"? Only to defend a hard pressed theory would any make this distinction. The following terms are all used *interchangeably* in reference to the Lord's coming to gather believers:

"The day of Christ" (Philippians 1:10).

"The day of Jesus Christ" (Philippians 1:6).

"The day of our Lord Jesus Christ" (1 Corinthians 1:8).

"The day of the Lord Jesus" (2 Corinthians 1:14).

"The day of the Lord" (1 Thessalonians 5:2).

We think it is inconsistent to try to make the last expression mean a different "Lord" or a different time than the other terms describe. The day of the Lord *is* the day of Christ in New Testament usage. And according to Paul, that day—when believers will be gathered unto him—will not come until AFTER the man of sin has been revealed!

WHEN DID IT BEGIN?

The teaching that there will be a secret coming of Christ *before* the appearance of the man of sin has been widely taught—and believed—in this century. Many fine Christians have accepted it with little or no investigation. But, as shocking as it may sound, this teaching was not the position of the early church, was not taught by the reformers, WAS NOT TAUGHT BY ANYONE UNTIL AROUND THE YEAR 1830! If this is true, then the secret, pre-tribulation rapture teaching is not a part of the true original faith that was once delivered unto the saints! It is not the old time gospel.

George Ladd, seminary professor, after making a survey of church history says: *"Every* church father who deals with this subject expects the *church* to suffer at the hands of Antichrist...we can find no trace of pretribulationism in the early church: and no modern pretribulationist has successfully proved that this particular doctrine was held by any of the church fathers or students of the word before the nineteenth century."[23]

This is quite a sweeping statement, but one which we believe will stand up under investigation. *The Didache,* one of the earliest pieces of Christian literature written after the New Testament, stated that the Antichrist would come, that many would be offended and lost, and the resurrection of the just would follow this time of woe.[24]

The *Epistle of Barnabas,* written about the same time, says: "When the Son comes, he will destroy the time of the Wicked one and will judge the godless"—thus placing the coming of Christ after the reign of the Wicked one, not before. He did not hold to an any moment return of Christ, for he expected the Roman empire to fall first.[25]

Justin Martyr (100-165) spoke of the coming of the Lord in these words: "He shall come from heaven with glory, when the man of apostasy, who speaks strange things against the most High, shall venture to do unlawful deeds on earth *against us Christians,* who, have learned the true worship of God from the law, and the word which went forth from Jerusalem by means of the apostles of Jesus." Christ "shall come from heaven with glory, accompanied by his angelic hosts, when also he shall raise the bodies of all men who have lived, and shall clothe those of the worthy with immortality."[26]

Irenaeus (130-202) spoke of "the resurrection of the just, which takes place *after* the coming of Antichrist ....But when this Antichrist shall have devastated all things in this world...*then* the Lord shall come from heaven in the clouds, in the glory of the Father, sending this man and those who follow him into the lake of fire; but bringing in for the righteous the times of the kingdom." He spoke of kings who "shall give their kingdom to the beast, and put the *church* to flight. After that they shall be destroyed by the coming of our Lord....In the *end* the church shall be suddenly caught up" and, having overcome, will be "crowned with incorruption."[27]

Tertullian (160-240) believed that Antichrist would rise to power and persecute the *church*. He affirmed it was customary for Christians to pray for a part in the resurrection to meet Christ at the *end* of the world.[28]

Hippolytus (170-236) spoke of the four empires of Daniel and that the breaking up of the fourth empire (which was then in power) would bring on the dreaded Antichrist who would persecute the *church*. He believed the second advent would be the time that the dead would be raised, Antichrist destroyed, and the saints glorified.[29]

Cyprian (200-258), a Christian bishop and martyr, believed Antichrist would reign, *after* which Christ would come at the *end* of the world.[30]

Lactantius (260-330) believed the Antichrist would reign over the world and afflict *the righteous,* but that God would send a Great King to rescue them, to destroy the wicked with fire and sword, to raise the dead and renew the world.[31]

Cyril (315-386), bishop of Jerusalem, wrote: "We believe in Him, who also ascended into the heavens, and sat down on the right hand of the Father, and shall come in glory to judge the quick and dead...at the *end* of this world, in *the last day.* For of this world there is to be an end, and this created world is to be re-made anew." It is evident, from various statements, that he believed Antichrist would come to power and persecute the church before the second coming of Christ.[32]

The essence of the teaching of these early writers is that Antichrist would persecute the church, that the coming of Christ would follow and bring an end to the reign of Antichrist, that the end of the world would be the time of resurrection when believers will be gathered to meet the Lord.

Those who hold the pre-tribulation position have sometimes quoted Irenaeus: "And therefore, when in the end the church shall be suddenly caught up it is said, 'There shall be tribulation such as has not been since the beginning neither shall be.' For this is the last contest of the righteous, in which, when they overcome, they are crowned with incorruption."[33] While it is true a part of this passage might seem to teach a pre-tribulation rapture, reading the whole passage shows this was not the intended meaning.

He spoke of tribulation as the "last" contest of the righteous and in overcoming they would be crowned. He spoke of the "end" as the time when the church will be suddenly caught up. We saw earlier that Irenaeus believed Antichrist would persecute the church and that after this Christ would come to reward the righteous and destroy the wicked. Certainly this was not the pre-tribulation position of dispensationalism.

A collection of visions, exhortations, and parables circulated around 150 A.D., known as the *Shepherd of Hermas*, has been cited. In one place the writer tells of meeting, and escaping from, what appeared to be a huge beast. A short distance on down the road, a virgin dressed in white told him that even as he escaped from the beast, those who truly repent would escape the great tribulation: "If then you prepare yourselves, and repent with all your heart and turn to the Lord, it will be possible for you to escape it, if your heart be pure and spotless."[34]

Though this passage speaks about escape from the great tribulation, we should not read into it things that are not there. Nothing is said about a secret rapture to take the church out of this world, nothing about two second comings of Christ or the accompanying dispensational teachings. Other passages of the *Shepherd of Hermas* present the view (commonly held by the early Christians) that tribulations and persecutions have a purifying effect on the church. Vision Two, for example, says: "Happy are ye who *endure* the great tribulation that is coming on, and happy are they who shall not deny their own life."[35] It would be quite difficult to build a pre-tribulation doctrine on this somewhat obscure book.

Looking on down through the centuries, there are certain names that stand out in Christian history: John Wyclif, John Huss, Martin Luther, Philipp Melanchthon, Huldreich Zwingli, William Tyndale, Nicholas Ridley, Hugh Latimer, John Foxe, Edwin Sandys, John Calvin, John Knox, King James, Isaac Newton, Thomas Newton, John Wesley. NONE of these men believed the church would be taken out before the appearance of Antichrist. They believed the church would suffer at the hands of Antichrist whose career would be ended by the return of Christ.

But today, many Christians have been taught the rapture will take them to heaven, before the Antichrist, and before Christ comes in power and glory. This teaching is of comparatively modern origin, dating from around 1830, and developing in the years that followed. Names associated with what was then a new teaching include Irving, McDonald, and Darby. First, we will notice the name of Edward Irving.

41

Born in Scotland in 1792, Irving was one of the most eloquent preachers of his time. In 1828 his open air meetings in Scotland drew crowds of 10,000 people. His church in London seated a thou-sand people and was packed week after week. When he wrote a tract inferring Jesus possessed a fallen human nature, however, a controversy arose among his people and he was removed from his pulpit in 1832, though the larger part of his congregation stood by him and sought for a new meeting place. An ecclesiastical trial in 1833 deprived him of his status as a clergyman in the Church of Scotland. His death the following year, 1834, at Glasgow, was attributed to tuberculosis and a broken heart.[36]

In September, 1830, Irving's journal, "The Morning Watch," carried an article which featured a two stage idea concerning the return of Christ. Some feel the seeds of this doctrine may have been a Spanish book, *The Coming of the Messiah in Glory and Majesty,* written by Manuel Lacunza, which Irving translated into English in 1827.[37] This book, originally published in 1812, said that "when the Lord returns from heaven to earth, upon his coming forth from heaven, and *much before* his arrival at the earth, he will give his orders, and send forth his commandment...with a shout...with the voice of the archangel, and with the trump of God. At this voice of the Son of God, those who hear it, shall forthwith arise."[38]

It is not clear just what he meant by "much before." Some believe he may have meant a few hours, which would be "much before" compared to the five or six minutes some were teaching. In any event, Lacunza linked the catching up of believers to passages such as Revelation 19, Matthew 24:30, and Revelation 1:7. This was still a long way from the now-popular dispensational teaching.

Though Lacunza was a Roman Catholic, Pope Leo XII placed his book on the list of prohibited books—and no wonder: Lacunza taught that the Roman Catholic priesthood would eventually become the two-horned beast of Revelation 13!

An acquaintance of Irving, Miss Margaret McDonald, is another name commonly associated with the early beginnings of the two stage idea. In a prophetic utterance given in the spring of 1830, she spoke of a coming of Christ that would be seen only by those whose eyes were spiritually open. She wrote an account of this and sent handwritten copies to various Christian leaders of the time. A book published by Robert Norton in 1840, *The Restoration of Apostles and Prophets In the Catholic Apostolic Church*, now very rare, gave a printed account of her revelation.[39] From this account, we will now quote the pertinent portions of this utterance:

Now there is distress of nations with perplexity, the seas and the waves roaring, men's hearts failing them for fear—now look out for the sign of the Son of man. Here I was made to stop and cry out, O it is not known what the sign of the Son of man is...I felt this needed to be revealed, and that there was great darkness and error about it; but suddenly what it was burst upon me with a glorious light. I saw it was just the Lord himself descending from Heaven with a shout, just the glorified man, even Jesus...men think that it will be something seen by the natural eye; but 'tis spiritual discernment that is needed....Only those who have the light of God within them will see the sign of his appearance....'tis only those that are alive in him that will be caught up to meet him in the air....I repeated frequently, but the spiritual temple must and shall be reared, and the fullness of Christ be poured into his body, and then shall we be caught up to meet him.

The church over the centuries had believed in the open, visible, glorious coming of the Lord. But in the McDonald utterance, something *not known* before was presented—a coming of the Lord *alone,* a coming *not seen* by the natural eye, a coming to catch up those who would be spiritually alive. Here then are hints of an earlier coming—before the open and visible coming of the Lord—but her exact position is not always clearly defined. Unlike the escape rapture theory in its present form, Miss McDonald went on to speak of great testing to befall the church.

> The Wicked will be revealed, with all power and signs and lying wonders, so that if it were possible the very elect will be deceived.—This is the fiery trial which is to try *us*.—It will be for the purging and purifying of the real members of the body of Jesus; but Oh it will be a fiery trial...I frequently said that night, and often since, now shall the awful sight of a false Christ be seen on this earth, and nothing but the living Christ in *us* can detect this awful attempt of the enemy to deceive....This is particularly the nature of the trial, through which those are to pass who will be counted worthy to stand before the Son of man....The trial of the *Church* is from *Antichrist*....Oh be filled with the Spirit....This is what we are at present made to pray much for, that speedily we may all be made ready to meet our Lord in the air—and it will be.

The Protestant churches at the time, and for centuries, held to historicism: that the Papacy was the man of sin or Antichrist who was making war against the saints, that the church was already in tribulations, that purifying trials were the lot of the church. They believed Revelation described events that spanned the centuries until the return of Christ. The famous Albury conferences taught that the church had now lived through the events of Revelation as far as chapter 16. (The idea that they were nearing a rapture at Revelation 4:1 was unknown!) Reading the entire wording of Margaret McDonald's utterance indicates her thinking was still that of the old historicist school of prophetic thought—but with a unique addition: the idea of a secret coming.

44

Soon the secret coming teaching was being taught among the group known as the Plymouth Brethren—to be accepted by some and rejected by others. In 1864, S.P. Tregelles, one of the Brethren that rejected this *new* teaching, wrote: "I am not aware that there was any definite teaching that there should be a secret rapture of the church at a secret coming until this was given forth as an 'utterance' in Mr. Irving's church from what was then received as being the voice of the Spirit. But whether any one ever asserted such a thing or not it was from that supposed revelation that the modern doctrine and the modern phraseology respecting it arose. It came, not from the Holy Scripture, but from that which falsely pretended to be the Spirit of God."[40]

Strangely enough, what at first was understood to be a new and special revelation—the teaching there would be a separate coming to rapture those that were ready—was soon to be dogmatically promoted AS THOUGH IT HAD ALWAYS BEEN THE ETERNAL TRUTH OF THE SCRIPTURES!

In the years that followed, the two stage teaching was developed further by John Nelson Darby (1800-1882). Irving apparently taught some kind of secret rapture, and there was the utterance of Margaret McDonald, but it was Darby who introduced it into the main current of prophetic interpretation. Darby was a  brilliant and well educated man whose writings on Biblical subjects number over 30 volumes of 600 pages each. He produced a translation of the Bible with notes, also wrote poems and hymns. In 1825, he was ordained a deacon in the Church of England. He later became a leader among the Plymouth Brethren, a movement which was composed largely of people who had become dissatisfied with the lethargic condition that prevailed in many of the churches. Though the movement had its beginning in Dublin, it was Plymouth, England, that became the center of their literature outreach, thus the name Plymouth Brethren.

Darby's biographers refer to him as "the father of modern dispensationalism." Many of the Plymouth Brethren accepted his dispensational teachings and were sometimes called Darbyites. But not all of the Plymouth Brethren accepted his position. B.W. Newton rejected the two-stage view as "nonsense." Other noted ministers of the time —among them George Muller, William Booth, and Charles Spurgeon—also opposed this theory as being unscriptural.

The secret rapture was introduced into the United States and Canada in the 1860s and 1870s, though there is some indication it may have been taught as early as the 1840s. Darby himself visited the United States six times. The "new" teaching was spreading.

Following the lead of Darby, the writings of Charles Henry Mackintosh (1820-1896), commonly known as C.H.M., helped spread the dispensational theory. William Blackstone wrote a book, *Jesus is Coming,* which taught the secret rapture position. It was distributed to ministers and people of various denominations throughout the country. But probably the biggest single factor that contributed to the spread of the pre-tribulation teaching was the printing of the *Scofield Reference Bible* in 1909.

SCOFIELD AND DISPENSATIONALISM

Cyrus Ingerson Scofield (1843-1921) was a soldier during the Civil War. Later he took up law and politics. During

the administration of President Grant, he was appointed U.S. Attorney to Kansas. In 1879, at St. Louis, he received Christ as savior. Three years later he became a Congregational minister. His first pastorate was at Dallas, Texas, where Dallas Theological Seminary still promotes the dispensational views he made popular through the notes of the *Scofield Reference Bible*. Whether he first heard about dispensationalism from Malachi Taylor, a member of the Plymouth Brethren, or J. H. Brooks, is not certain. He was definitely influenced by Darby, whom he considered "the most profound Bible student of modern times."[41]

Some have written about Scofield's divorce (from a Roman Catholic woman) and remarriage. Some believe the "Dr." in front of his name was self-given. Others have questioned some of his financial dealings and membership in a prestigious club. We will leave a discussion of those things, now long past, to others. In many ways Scofield stood for sound principles of evangelical Christianity. But his dispensationalism, being of comparatively modern origin, should be rejected.

Because of the Scofield Bible, many were led to believe in a secret rapture. Oswald J. Smith was one of them. But later he would write: "Now, after years of study and prayer, I am absolutely convinced that there will be no rapture *before* the tribulation...I believed the other theory simply because I was taught it by W.E. Blackstone in his book *Jesus is Coming,* the *Scofield Reference Bible* and prophetic conferences and Bible schools; but when I began to search the scriptures for myself I discovered that there is not a single verse in the Bible that upholds the pre-tribulation theory."[42]

Philip Mauro (1859-1952), an outstanding Biblical scholar, had a similar experience. "It is mortifying to remember," he wrote, "that I not only held and taught these novelties myself, but that I even enjoyed a complacent sense of superiority because thereof, and regarded with feelings of pity and contempt those who had not received the 'new light'and were unacquainted with this up-to-date method of 'rightly dividing the word of truth'....The time came...when the inconsistencies and self-contradictions of the system itself, and above all, the impossibility of reconciling its main positions with the plain statements of the Word of God, became so glaringly evident that I could not do otherwise than to renounce it."[43]

G. Campbell Morgan (1863-1945), when asked if he believed in the two-stage view, said this about his experience: "Emphatically not! I know this view very well. In the earlier years of my ministry I taught it and incorporated it in one of my books *(God's Method With Man).* But further study so convinced me of the error of this teaching that I actually went to the expense of buying the plates from the publishers and destroying them. The idea of a separate and secret coming of Christ is a vagary of prophetic interpretation without any Biblical basis whatsoever."[44]

In all due respect to those who still hold the secret rapture teaching—some dear friends and fellow ministers being among that number—it is our sincere conviction that it should be rejected, first, because it lacks solid scriptural support, and, secondly, because of its comparatively recent origin. Though the secret rapture position still receives a lot of publicity, there are many within the body of Christ who are taking a second look at the rapture question. There is a distinct turning back to the original, apostolic, historical position.

For God so loved the world,

he gave his only Son,

To die on Calvary's tree,

from sin to set me free.

One day he's coming back,

what glory that will be!

Wonderful his love to me![45]

NOTES

1. Oral Roberts, *How to be Personally Prepared for the Second Coming of Christ* (Tulsa: Oral Roberts Evangelistic Association, 1967), p.34.

2. Jesse F. Silver, *The Lord's Return* (New York: Revell, 1914), p.260.

3. Herschel W. Ford, *Seven Simple Sermons on the Second Coming* (Grand Rapids: Zondervan, 1946), p.51.

4. Hal Lindsey, *The Late Great Planet Earth* (Grand Rapids: Zondervan Publishing House, 1970), p.143.

5. G.S. Bishop, *The Doctrine of Grace*, p.341.

6. C.I. Scofield, *Scofield Reference Bible* (New York: Oxford University Press, 1917), p.1016.

7. Hal Lindsey, *op. cit.*, p.111.

8. Frank M. Boyd, *Ages and Dispensations* (Springfield: Gospel Publishing House, 1955), p.60.

9. William W. Orr, *Antichrist, Armageddon, and the End of the World* (Grand Rapids: Dunham Publishing Company, 1966), p.9.

10. Carl Sabiers, *Where Are the Dead?*, pp.123,124.

11. Oswald Smith, *Tribulation or Rapture—Which?* (London: The Sovereign Grace Advent Testimony), p.9.

12. *The Pulpit Commentary* (Grand Rapids: Eerdmans Publishing Company, reprint 1950), Vol.22, p.12.

13. *Ibid.*, Vol. 3, p.534.

14. Matthew Henry, *Matthew Henry's Commentary* (New York: Fleming H. Revell Company, reprint of 1721 edition), p.874. Cf. Job 15:15; Psalms 89:5,7; Daniel 8:13; 4:13.

15. Oswald Smith, *op. cit.*, p.10.

16. William R. Kimball, *The Rapture, A Question of Timing* (Grand Rapids: Baker Book House, 1985), p.179, quoted from *Christianity Today*, August 1959.

17. Pat Robertson, *Answers to 200 of Life's Most Probing Questions* (Nashville: Thomas Nelson Publishers, 1984), pp.155,156.

18. Wilfrid C. "Will" Meloon, *Eschaton*, issue XVI (Orange City, FL: 1979).

19. Scofield, *op. cit.*, p.1334.

20. M.R. De Haan, *Thirty-five Simple Studies on the Major Themes in Revelation* (Grand Rapids: Zondervan, 1946), p.61.

21. Scofield, *op. cit.*, p.1348.

22. *Ibid.*, p.1212.

23. George E. Ladd, *The Blessed Hope* (Grand Rapids: Eerdmans, 1956), p.31.

24. *Ibid.*

25. Barnabas, in *Ante-Nicene Fathers*, Vol. 1, pp. 146,138.

26. Justin, *Dialogue with Trypho*, chapter 52.

27. Irenaeus, *Against Heresies*, 35:1, 30:4, 26:1, 29:1.

28. Tertullian, *On the Resurrection of the Flesh*, chapter Twenty-two.

29. Hippolytus, *Treatise on Christ and Antichrist*, chapters 66,67.

30. Cyprian, *Epistle 55*.

31. Lactantius, *The Divine Institutes*, Vol.7.

32. *The Catechetical Lectures of St. Cyril*, Lecture 15.

33. Irenaeus, *op. cit.*, 5:29.

34. *Hermas*, Vision 4, chapter 2.

35. *Ibid.*, Vision 2, chapter 2.

36. LeRoy E. Froom, *The Prophetic Faith of Our Fathers* (Washington: Review and Herald, 1945), Vol.3, p.516.

37. John L. Bray, *The Origin of the Pre-Tribulation Rapture Teaching* (Lakeland, FL: John L. Bray Ministry, Inc., 1982).

38. Manuel de Lacunza, *The Coming of Messiah in Glory and Majesty* (London: translated by Irving, 1827), Vol.1, p.99.

39. Quoted by Dave MacPherson, *The Great Rapture Hoax* (Fletcher, NC: New Puritan Library, 1983), pp.125-128.

40. S.P. Tregelles, *The Hope of Christ's Second Coming* (London: Samuel Bagster and Sons, 1864), pp.34-37.

41. *Dr. C.I. Scofield's Question Box*, (Chicago: The Bible Institute Colportage Association, compiled by Ella E. Pohle), p.93.

42. Smith, *op. cit.*, pp.2,3.

43. Kimball, *op. cit.*, pp.177,178.

44. *Ibid.*

45. Frances Townsend, *For God so Loved the World* (1938).

All scriptures that teach the second coming of Christ will be in two stages are listed on this page:

MORE INFORMATION...

Now you have read *THE SECRET RAPTURE—Is it Scriptural?* (based on part one of the large book *GREAT PROPHECIES OF THE BIBLE*).

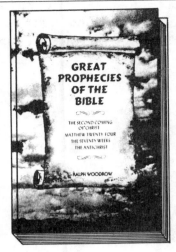

Does the New Testament ever mention a seven year tribulation period?

Is the great tribulation mentioned in Matthew 24 future or fufilled?

What is the abomination of desolation? Are expressions about the sun, moon, and stars being darkened literal or figurative?

Does the fig tree symbolize the modern nation of Israel?

Daniel's seventieth week—is it future or fulfilled? Does a gap of 2,000 years follow the 69th week? Is the subject of the prophecy Christ or Antichrist?

Will the Antichrist make a covenant with the Jews, allowing them to offer animal sacrifices in a rebuilt temple at Jerusalem?

Is the falling away and rise of the man of sin future or fulfilled?

All of these questions are discussed in detail in the large, complete book, *GREAT PROPHECIES OF THE BIBLE*.

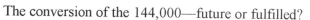